History Of
TOYS AND GAMES

Peter Chrisp

WAYLAND

Books in the series

History of Canals
History of Fairs and Markets
History of Food and Cooking
History of Toys and Games

Series editor: Sarah Doughty
Book editor: Ruth Raudsepp
Designer: Michael Leaman
Production controller: Carol Stevens

First published in 1996 by Wayland (Publishers) Limited
61 Western Road, Hove, East Sussex BN3 1JD, England.

British Library Cataloguing in Publication Data
Chrisp, Peter
History of Toys and Games. – (History of Series)
I. Title II Series
790. 192209

ISBN 0-7502-1679-4

Picture Acknowledgements
AKG London 29; Ancient Art and Architecture Collection 10, 12, 14 (bottom); APM Studios 15, 42 (top);
Bodleian Library 13 (top and bottom); Bridgeman Art Library 7, 16, 17, 25; British Library 11, 18 (top), 26, 28;
CM Dixon 9; English Heritage Photographic Library 8; Gloucester Cathedral 14; Hulton Deutsch Collection 27, 37, 41 (top);
London Toy and Model Museum 6; Mary Evans Picture Library 20, 23, 32 (top); Michael Holford 4, 31 (bottom), 33;
National Trust Photographic Library 21, 30, 35; Peter Newark's Historical Pictures 18, 19;
Robert Opie Collection 24, 31 (top), 34, 38, 40;7, 16, 17, 25; Topham 36, 39; Tullie House Museum, Carlisle 7;
Victoria and Albert Museum 22; Yorkshire Museum 5. The remaining pictures are from the Wayland Picture Library.

Typeset by Michael Leaman Design Partnership
Printed and bound in England
by B P C Paulton Books

Contents

Roman Britain

Children have been playing with toys for thousands of years, yet very few ancient toys have survived. This is because toys were never meant to last for a long time – the very word 'toy' originally meant something small and unimportant. Children used toys until they got broken and then threw them away. Since they were mostly made from wood or rags, they quickly rotted and disappeared.

The Romans

The story of toys and games in Britain begins with the arrival of the Romans, who began to conquer the island in AD 43. For almost the next 400 years, Britain was part of the vast Roman Empire.

Unlike earlier peoples in Britain, the Romans wrote books, which have many descriptions of children's games. Roman artists also made stone carvings, mosaics and wall-paintings, showing scenes of daily life.

◀ *A pull-along wooden horse from a child's grave in Egypt, another part of the Roman Empire. Such toys must have been common everywhere. This toy, almost 2,000 years old, survived because Egypt is such a dry place.*

Children's Tombs

'May the turf lie lightly on her and may you, earth, not be a heavy weight upon her. For she was no great weight on you.'

This is from a poem, written by the poet Martial, on the death of a five-year-old girl called Erotion. In Roman times, the death of young children was a common event. This was because their were no cures for the many childhood diseases during Roman times.

Grieving parents often buried their children with favourite toys, such as rattles and dolls. Occasionally, these toys have been found.

Ball Games

The Romans played with several different types of ball – heavy ones, made from wood, and light ones, stuffed with feathers or horsehair. These balls did not bounce, so ball games mainly involved throwing and catching.

▲ *A little boy plays with his pet bird, carved on a woman's tombstone from Carlisle.*

The best-known ball game was called 'trigon'. Three players, each with a ball, stood in a triangle. Each then threw the ball to the player on their right, while trying to catch the ball thrown from the left. Trigon was played by adults as well as children, as a way of keeping fit.

Little Fronto, a Roman Toddler

A Roman writer called Marcus Cornelius Fronto sent a letter to his son-in-law, describing his grandson, little Fronto:

'The one word your little Fronto continually says is '*da!*' (Give me!). I hand over whatever I can ... He shows signs of his grandfather's character too: he is particularly greedy for grapes ... He is also very keen on little birds: he loves young chicks, pigeons and sparrows ... Right from my earliest childhood, I too was enthralled by these birds.'

Children like little Fronto had their own pet animals – birds, dogs and mice, which were sometimes harnessed to pull tiny toy carts. There were also bigger carts, pulled by pet goats or donkeys, which the children could ride in.

▶*A Roman gladiator doll. Holes at the shoulders and hips show that he once had moving limbs. He probably held a sword and shield.*

Dolls

Girls played with dolls, carved from wood or bone, or made from pottery. All three types of doll have been found in girls' graves. One pottery doll from Rome had a rough bald head, which at one time was probably covered with human hair.

Before marrying, girls were expected to offer up their dolls to Venus, the goddess of love. They took their toys to her temple, or placed them in front of a small statue of Venus, kept in a household shrine. Putting aside their toys like this was a sign that they were now grown-ups.

Gladiator Dolls

Boys also played with dolls. Like the doll 'Action Man' today, Roman boys' dolls took the form of fighting figures. They were gladiators, men who fought each other to the death for public entertainment. Successful gladiators were like sports or film stars and they had their own fans.

Tops

Boys played with wooden hoops and spinning tops, described by the Roman poet Virgil as:

'... a whip-top whirling under the twisted lash, which boys intent on their sport drive in a large circuit round some empty court.'

There were different ways of getting a top to spin. Some had long spindles on top, which could be given a sharp twist with the hand. The top described here was set spinning with a length of cord. This was wrapped around it and then jerked quickly away. It buzzed as it glided across the floor. The boys kept it going by striking it with a whip.

▲ *This tombstone, from York, shows the family of a Roman soldier. His son and daughter, who both died before they were two years old, are holding balls to play with.*

◀ *Long after Roman times, children were still playing in the street with wooden spinning tops. This is a Victorian painting.*

Saturnalia

Particular times of the year have always been linked with their own customs and games. On 17 December every year, the Romans began to celebrate the Saturnalia, the midwinter **festival** of their god Saturn. Like our April Fools' Day, it was a time for playing tricks. The normal rules of life were forgotten for a few days. Men dressed up in women's clothes, and slaves were allowed to make fun of their masters and mistresses.

Gifts for Saturnalia

At parties, people gave each other Saturnalia presents, such as small pottery dolls for the children. The writer Suetonius described some presents given by the Emperor Augustus:

'He playfully varied the value of his gifts. They might consist of rich clothing and gold or silver plate ... or merely lengths of goat-hair cloth, or sponges, or pokers.'

To claim your present, you first had to pick a ticket out of a bowl. This ticket would have a misleading description of the gift written on it. Another writer, Petronius, listed some ticket descriptions and gifts:

'"Old man's wit'– dry salt biscuits came up ...
"Flies and a fly trap" was raisins and a jar of honey ...
We laughed for ages.'

◀ *These Roman die, and the cups for shaking them, were found at a Roman fort at Corbridge in Northumberland.*

◄ *It was at dinner parties like this that the Romans celebrated Saturnalia, gambling with dice.*

Die

Some people spent the whole of Saturnalia gambling with die, a game described in a letter by the Emperor Augustus:

'We gambled like old men all through the meal, and until yesterday turned into today. Anyone who threw the Dog [two ones] or a six, put a silver piece down; and anyone who threw Venus, when each of the dice shows a different number, scooped the lot.'

The Bronze Fly

In the late second century AD, a Greek writer called Pollux, who was tutor to the family of the Roman Emperor, wrote a book in which he described the games of the time. This is his description of a form of 'blindman's buff', called 'the bronze fly':

'They bind a boy's eyes with a headband, and he is turned round and round, calling out, "I will chase the bronze fly." His friends answer, "You will chase him but you won't catch him." They hit him with paper whips until he catches them.'

Playing with Pebbles, Nuts and Bones

Roman children were happy playing with the simplest things, such as pebbles and nuts. One way of saying that someone was no longer a child was that they had 'stopped playing with nuts'.

Nuts were used like marbles, or in a guessing game called '*par impar*' (even or odd). One child held out a fist, hiding the nuts, and the others had to guess whether there was an odd or even number.

▲ *Greek women play knucklebones. Sculptures and wall-paintings show that this game was especially popular with girls and young women.*

Girls and young women played a game with the knucklebones of a sheep. It was described by the writer, Pollux:

'Knucklebones are thrown up into the air, and an attempt is made to catch them on the back of the hand. If you are only partially successful, you have to pick up the knucklebones which have fallen to the ground, without letting fall those already on your hand.'

This game is still played today, but with plastic or metal 'jacks' rather than real knucklebones.

▶ *Sheep's knucklebones could be used like die. The different shaped sides of the bones were given different values.*

Bucca

Children played a guessing game with their fingers called 'bucca'. The writer Petronius described the game:

'Trimalchio told the boy to climb on his back. Without delay, the boy climbed on his back, and slapped him on the shoulders with his hand, laughing and calling out "*Bucca, Bucca, quot sunt hic*?" (Bigmouth, Bigmouth, how many are there?)'

The person playing the horse had to guess how many fingers the rider was holding out. If he guessed correctly, they swapped places. Although it doesn't sound very exciting, 'bucca' turned out to be one of the most popular games in history. Long after the ancient Romans themselves were forgotten, their game was still being played by children all over Europe. Here's how it was described in 1856:

▲ *Playing 'bucca', the ancient Roman game in about 1600.*

'The boy who plays the Buck gives a back with his head down, and rests his hands on some wall or paling in front of him. The boy who mounts him then cries "Buck! Buck! How many horns do I hold up?"'

This game was still being played in the north of England in the 1960s, where it was called 'bugs'. The children playing it had no idea that their game was 2,000 years old, or that its name came from Latin.

The Middle Ages

Roman rule broke down in the fifth century AD. Over the next 600 years, Britain was invaded and settled by new peoples – Anglo-Saxons from northern Germany, Vikings from Scandinavia and Normans from France.

▶ Throughout the Middle Ages in northern Europe, whole villages joined in the wild dance around the maypole.

These different peoples brought their own customs and festivals. The Anglo-Saxons, for example, had a midwinter festival called Yule, and a spring festival in honour of their god, Eostre. This gives us our word 'Easter'.

▼ 'Blindman's buff' was a rough game in the Middle Ages. The blindfolded woman is being whacked by the others with knotted lengths of cloth. The word 'buff' means a blow.

The Anglo-Saxons celebrated festivals with feasts, dances and games, such as 'blindman's buff' and 'leapfrog'. When they adopted the Christian faith, Anglo-Saxons kept many of their old festival customs. The difference was that they were now celebrating in honour of Christ rather than their old gods.

Holy Days

In the Middle Ages, the year was full of religious festivals. As well as the biggest events, Christmas and Easter, there were over a hundred saints' days. People did not work on **'holy days'**, as saints' days and Sundays were called. This is where our word 'holiday' comes from.

Holy days were times for fun and games. In the 1170s, a writer called William Fitzstephen described them:

'In the holy days all the summer the youths are exercised in archery, running, jumping, wrestling, slinging the stone ... the maidens dance, and until the moon rises, the earth is shaken with flying feet.'

Different games and pastimes were linked with different festivals. On St John's Eve, at midsummer, young people jumped over bonfires. On May Day, they went into the woods to collect flowering branches to decorate their homes. This was called 'bringing in the May', welcoming the arrival of Summer. The day was spent playing games and dancing around a **maypole**.

▼ *Children enjoying a glove-puppet show. Like Mr Punch, the puppet on the left has a huge club. He may be the ancient Greek hero and strong man, Hercules.*

The Big Fairs

On important holy days, big fairs were held where goods were sold and entertainments could be seen. There were jugglers, stilt walkers, acrobats, dancing bears and puppet shows. Children visiting the fairs could buy simple wooden toys called 'fairings'. These included dolls, wind toys, tops, rattles, drums and **hobby horses**. There were also toys you could eat, such as gingerbread men.

Shrove Tuesday Games

William Fitzstephen described how London schoolboys celebrated Shrove Tuesday, the festival before Lent:

▲ *A ball game, from a carving in Gloucester Cathedral.*

▼ *Skating on a frozen river in Flanders in 1558. A small child, too young to skate, is pushing himself along on a homemade sledge. In the background, a type of ice hockey is being played.*

'The schoolboys bring fighting cocks to their masters, and the whole morning is set apart to watch the cocks do battle in the schools ... After dinner, all the youths go into the fields to play at the ball.'

Football was played all over the country on Shrove Tuesday. All the young men in a village would take part, kicking a pig's bladder wrapped in leather or a small hard ball over the fields. There were no rules, and players were often badly hurt. In 1531, the writer Sir Thomas Elyot, complained that 'football is nothing but beastly fury and extreme violence.'

Winter Fun

Britain's weather was colder in the Middle Ages than it is today. Rivers and ponds often froze over in winter. William Fitzstephen described some winter games:

'Swarms of young men go forth to play games on the ice. Some, gaining speed in their run, with feet set well apart, slide sideways over a vast expanse of ice. Others make seats out of a large lump of ice, and while one sits on it, others with linked hands run before and drag him along behind them.'

◄ These children are playing nine men's morris, one of the most popular games of the Middle Ages.

Nine Men's Morris

Nine men's morris was a board game that was played all over Britain in the Middle Ages. Two players marked out squares and dots, cutting them into the earth or drawing them on stone or slate with chalk. Each had nine pebbles or bits of chalk called 'men'. The players took turns at placing their men on the dots. The aim was to get three men into a straight row, and to stop the other player doing the same.

When all the men were on the board, the players took turns at moving them, one place at a time. When a player got three men into a row, he was allowed to 'capture' (remove) one of the other player's men. The game continued until one side's men had all been captured.

Children's Games in the 1560s

This wonderful painting, by Peter Brueghel, shows more than 200 children playing over eighty different games. Imagine the noise they must be making!

Brueghel lived in Flanders, a country now split between France, Belgium and The Netherlands. The games in this painting were also known in Britain at the time. Many of them, such as knucklebones, had been played since Roman times.

▼ *Some of the children are playing blindman's buff and leapfrog. Can you find them?*

Toys

The only specially made toys in the picture are dolls, windmills, tops, stilts and the hobby horse. Most of the toys are the sort of objects found lying around in a village, such as knucklebones, hoops from the barrels, blown-up pigs' bladders, pebbles and cherry stones. The girl at the very bottom is happy making mud pies with a stick.

Let's Pretend

Some of the games are 'let's pretend', in which children copy the behaviour of adults. At the bottom-left, a doll wrapped in a blue cloth is carried in a mock christening procession. You can see another procession right in the centre of the picture. This is a pretend wedding, and the girl wearing the crown is the bride.

The girl at the bottom-right is pretending to be a shopkeeper. She has homemade scales, a paper scoop and a brick representing a cake, bread or cheese. The boys next to her are playing 'bucca', the old Roman game described on page 11.

Cockstride

In the centre-right, a strange game is being played. A boy, wearing a red cap over his face is standing with his legs apart. Meanwhile, other boys are throwing their hats between his legs. This was called 'cockstride' and the boy with his legs apart is playing the cockerel. In the next stage of the game, the cockerel, his face still covered, has to crawl forward and pick up a hat. The unlucky boy whose hat has been chosen then has to run between the others, dodging their blows. This game was still being played in the 1890s, but it disappeared in the twentieth century when boys stopped wearing hats.

When Games were Banned

▲ *This picture shows the character of Christmas, driven out of the city by the Puritans, welcomed by the country folk.*

▼ *Puritan families spent their Sundays reading the Bible together. Many Puritans would not have let their children play with a hobby horse, as this child is doing.*

'Where God calleth it his holy Sabbath, the multitude call it their revelling day, which day is spent in bull-baitings, bowling, dicing, carding, dancings, drunkenness ...'

These words come from a sermon, preached at Blandford Forum, in 1571. The preacher, William Kethe, was explaining why he believed that it was wrong to play games on a Sunday. Kethe was a **Puritan**, someone who wanted to make people live a more religious life.

The Puritans hated the idea of special holy days, such as saints' days. To Puritans, all days were holy. They said that it was everyone's duty to work hard for six days and then spend Sunday praying, listening to sermons, reading the Bible and praising God.

A Puritan Childhood

Richard Baxter grew up in a Puritan family in the 1620s. In his autobiography, he described how his family spent their Sundays reading the Bible together. Meanwhile, he could hear his fellow villagers having fun in the street, dancing around a maypole:

'We could not read the Scripture in our family without the great disturbance of the tabor (drum) and pipe and noise in the street.'

Richard often felt tempted to join them:

'But when I heard them call my father Puritan it did much to cure me ... for I considered my father's exercise in reading the Scripture was better than theirs.'

Laws against Games

In the 1640s, there was a civil war between the forces of King Charles I and his parliament. Many people on the parliamentary side were Puritans.

After the parliament's victory over the king, Puritans were able to pass laws against Sunday games. All over the country, maypoles were pulled down. **Morris dancing** was forbidden. In some places, people were arrested for playing football.

The Puritans even abolished Christmas, ordering shops to stay open on that day. In the town of Elgin in Scotland, troops went from house to house, making sure that people weren't cooking a Christmas goose.

▲ *The Puritans were horrified by people who spent their Sundays singing and dancing.*

It was very hard to make people obey the laws against games. Just before Shrove Tuesday, 1660, the Bristol authorities announced a ban on the ancient sports of 'cock-throwing, dog-tossing and football in the streets.' The people of Bristol rioted in protest.

Toy Makers and Toy Sellers

Until the end of the Middle Ages, toys were almost all home-made. In the winter months, when there was little farm work to be done, people relaxed by the fire, carving dolls and animals from wood. Some took their toys to sell at the fairs, or sold them from door to door. For these people, making toys was a hobby rather than a full-time job.

Beginnings of the Toy Industry

In the 1400s, a real toy industry appeared in the forests of southern Germany. This area was rich in softwood, a tree whose wood is easy to carve. There were skilled wood carvers here, who made figures of Christ and the saints to decorate churches. At Christmas, they carved animals for scenes of Christ's birth in the stable. By the 1400s, some of the wood carvers had stopped making religious figures and instead they carved toys for children.

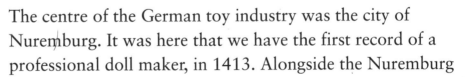

The centre of the German toy industry was the city of Nuremburg. It was here that we have the first record of a professional doll maker, in 1413. Alongside the Nuremburg carvers, there were also merchants who bought their toys and took them to sell at the great fairs across Germany. The German toys were so well made that they were soon being sold in fairs in other countries, all over Europe.

▼ *This 1491 German picture is the earliest image of professional doll makers.*

Guilds

German craftspeople belonged to organizations called **guilds**. These laid down strict rules about the work their members could do. Painters, for example, were not allowed to carve wood. Similarly, wood carvers were not supposed to paint their toys. A toy might have to go through several workshops before it was finished.

Different guilds belonged to different ranks of society. The carvers of religious figures looked down on the doll makers; and in turn, the doll makers looked down on the spoon makers.

The highest rank was formed by the skilled metalworkers, the silversmiths and clock makers. They made expensive toys for the royal families of Europe. In the 1660s, King Louis XIV of France asked a Nuremburg silversmith, Gottfried Hautsch, to make a set of over a hundred silver soldiers for his young son. Hautsch spent four years working on them. They were **clockwork,** and so cleverly made that they could march across the floor and take aim. Unfortunately, they have not survived. They must have looked wonderful!

▼ *This painting of the 1750s shows Arabella Stuart, aged just under two years old, clutching a beautifully made doll, which may well have come from Germany or The Netherlands.*

New Materials

Carving dolls out of wood is a long, slow job. As the demand for German toys grew throughout Europe, the toy makers had to find quicker methods and new materials.

One of the new materials was called *pappenseuch* (soaked paper). Soaked paper pulp was pushed into a mould of a doll's head. Once it had dried, the mould was removed and the doll's face was painted by hand.

Toy makers tried many different combinations of soaked paper, plaster, and flour or glue. The mixture, called **'composition'**, was perfect for making large numbers of dolls' heads quickly. The heads were painted or coated with wax for a smooth, skin-like finish.

Machinery

Toy making was also speeded up by machinery, which was driven by flowing rivers or steam. Some machines drove **lathes** for carving wood. Others stamped out toys from sheets of tin. Once the factories arrived, toy making became one of Germany's most important industries.

◀ *A composition, or paste doll, from the early 1800s. The body is stuffed cloth, like a rag doll. Only the head is made of composition.*

Working from Home

Many toy makers continued to work from home, carving toys by hand. Children, parents and grandparents all worked together. They were paid tiny wages by the toy merchants.

The carving of simple toys was taught and passed on to each generation. In 1879, a French traveller visited an old lady who lived in the town of Oberammergau, where Noah's Arks were made. She had been taught by her mother to carve six animals:

'They were a dog, cat, wolf, sheep, goat and elephant. She had cut these all her life and could not cut anything else. It was her trade. And she had taught her daughter and grand-daughter as a life's work to cut these six animals. In one house they will perhaps paint nothing but grey horses with black spots, in another only red horses with white spots.'

▲ *Young girls hard at work making dolls in the 1870s.*

Child Labour

Poor children worked long hours making toys for wealthy children to play with. They could not afford to own the toys they made themselves. This gave rise to an English rhyme:

'The children of England take pleasure in breaking
What the children of Holland take pleasure in making.'

In fact, toy making was a very boring job, and the wooden animals were nicknamed 'misery toys' by their makers.

Toy Shops

Until the early 1700s, most toys were bought at fairs or from street pedlars. They could also be found at mercers' shops. These were shops that sold fabrics, such as silks and ribbons.

The first proper toy shops appeared in Britain in the 1700s. They sold British-made toys alongside toys from Germany and The Netherlands. British toys were usually sturdy wooden objects, such as wheelbarrows and hobby horses.

▲ *Inside a Victorian toy shop. Pull-along horses were still very popular in the nineteenth century, as they had been since Roman times.*

Street Pedlars

Street pedlars carried on selling toys until the twentieth century. They wandered the countryside on foot, carrying their goods in a wicker basket.

▶ *Pedlars were such a common sight that British toy makers made pedlar dolls, like these.*

Advertising Toys

Toy shops advertised their goods with handbills – printed sheets of paper handed out in the street. This poem, from a nineteenth-century handbill, gives an idea of the range of toys sold:

'A Shovel, a Barrow, a Rake or a Spade,
You'll find at our counter the best that are made.
The New Eagle Kite, with Traps, Balls and Bats,
German Boxes of Toys, and Musical Cats,
The GAME of AUNT SALLY, an English farm,
And pop-guns from France that will do you no harm ...
Such beautiful Dolls that will open their Eyes,
You may wash, comb and dress them and not fear their cries ...
So dear little friends, just bear this in mind,
'Tis at H. PIEROTTI'S these wonders you'll find.'

▼ *The Lowther Arcade in the 1890s where many toy shops could be found.*

Lowther Arcade

This is a picture of London's Lowther Arcade, where the best toy shops in Britain could be found in the 1890s. There was a wonderful variety of toys here. There were shops owned by Swiss, French and German businesses, which all stocked toys from their own countries.

The families in this picture all look wealthy, but poorer children also liked to come to the Arcade and look at all the toys. It was such a famous sight that it had a popular song written about it, 'The Tin Gee-Gee':

'I was strolling down the Lowther Arcade,
That's a place for children's toys,
Where you can purchase a dolly or a spade
For good little girls and boys.'

Games in the Street

After 1700, an interest in folklore developed. The songs, beliefs and pastimes of ordinary people, passed down from one generation to another, were recorded by writers. These writers described the games that children played in the streets of Britain.

Children played hundreds of different games. Some, such as 'hide and seek' and 'he,' were based on chasing and seeking. Others were games of strength, such as 'tug of war'. There were also games based on guessing, racing, pretending, skipping and clapping.

▼ *This picture of 'thread the needle' comes from* A Little Pretty Pocket Book *(1744), one of the first books written especially for children.*

Thread the Needle

'Thread the needle' was a game in which several children joined hands to form a line. Two at one end then raised their hands to form an arch, the eye of the needle. Then the child at the other end of the line ran through the arch, leading everyone else, until the two forming the arch had to twist round and follow. At this stage, the pair now leading the line formed a new arch for everyone to run through.

As they rushed through the arch, the children sang songs, such as 'The tailor's blind and he can't see, so we must thread the needle.'

The game was played by adults as well as children. This is how it was played in Penzance, Cornwall, in 1801:

'Male and female, young, middle-aged and old ... take hands, and forming a long string, run violently through every street, lane and alley, crying 'An eye! An eye! An eye!' At last they stop suddenly; and an eye to this enormous needle being opened by the last two in the string ... the thread of populace run under and through; and continue to repeat the same, till weariness ... sends them home to bed.'

Clapping Games

Since the 1700s, girls have played clapping games to rhymes. The rhymes provided the beat for the clapping and the aim was to go on for as long as possible without making a mistake. Different hands were clapped one after another.

▼ *Poor boys playing marbles in the 1850s, captured by a new invention, photography. Look how heavily patched their trousers are! They had to last a long time, and playing marbles did not help.*

Here's a clapping rhyme from 1875:

'My mother said (clap)
That I never should (clap)
Play with the gypsies
(clap) In the wood (clap)
Because she said (clap)
That if I did (clap) She'd
smack my bottom (clap)
With a saucepan lid (clap)'

Skipping

In the 1600s, skipping was a boy's game. See if you can find the skipping boy in this picture below showing Dutch children playing (1642). The picture also shows why girls didn't skip. Imagine trying to skip in one of these long heavy dresses!

Skipping became a girls' game in the nineteenth century when shorter skirts arrived. As with clapping, songs and rhymes provided a rhythm: 'Cups and saucers, plates and dishes, my old man wears calico breeches.' In a typical game, two girls twirled the rope faster and faster, repeating 'Pepper, salt, mustard, cider, vinegar' while a third girl skipped.

Old Man in the Well

Some games were like little plays, in which children took on different roles. One acting game was 'Old Man in the Well', first described in the 1880s. In this game, the children had to pretend to be a mother, her children and a frightening old man.

The game begins with the children asking their mother for bread and butter. She tells them to wash their hands first. They go to the

► *Dutch children playing, from* A Book of Emblems *by Jacob Cats, dated about 1642.*

well, a dark corner, only to see the old man, crouching as if about to pounce. They rush back shouting, 'Mother! There's an old man in the well!'

Refusing to believe them, mother sends them back to the well. Again they see the old man and rush back. Eventually, they persuade her to go to the well herself. She peers down and sees the old man, who jumps up with a terrifying shriek. He chases the others, who run away screaming. Whoever he catches becomes the next old man.

▲ *In the 1600s, boys enjoyed skipping on their own. More complicated skipping games were invented later, by girls.*

This game was played all over Britain and was called different names in different places. In Cornwall it was 'Ghost at the Well,' and in Aberdeen, 'Devil among the Dishes.' Nobody knows when the game was first played or who invented it. The game was popular for the same reason that horror films are, because we all enjoy being scared sometimes. Here's one woman's memory of the game:

'The queer thing was that we were all *really* terrified by the old man in the well. We knew he was a playmate, we had even been him ourselves ... But the old man was terrifying ... In fact, we seldom played the game, it scared us so much.'

In the Victorian Nursery

During the long reign of Queen Victoria (1837–1901), there were big differences between the lives of poor and rich children. Until the law was changed in the 1870s, children as young as six were working long hours in factories and coal mines. Such working children had few, if any, toys. In any case, they were usually too tired after their work to play games.

The children of the rich led very different lives. They spent their early years living in the nursery, which was often at the top of the house. This was so that the noise of the children playing did not disturb their parents. There was a saying that children should be seen but not heard.

▼ *This Victorian nursery is in a large house called Erddig, near Wrexham in Wales.*

The children were looked after by their nursemaid or nanny, who washed them, fed them, played with them and took them for walks in the park. In the late afternoon, she brought them downstairs to sit with their parents for a short time. Many children felt closer to their nanny than they did to their parents.

Toys that Teach

Victorian parents thought that toys should not simply be fun to play with, but that they should also teach. Children could learn to spell using building blocks decorated with letters. They could learn about geography, history and the Bible through jigsaw puzzles and board games. They could even learn good behaviour by playing a board game called 'Virtue Rewarded and Vice Punished.'

▲ *'What d'ye buy?,' a game that taught about different types of shop and the goods that they sold.*

Dolls' Houses

Dolls' houses, also called 'baby houses', were also bought as teaching toys. They were said to be useful for preparing girls for 'household management', the job of running a big house and giving orders to all the servants. This 1890s dolls' house belonged to a girl called Amy Miles. It is full of details of life in a big Victorian home. The nursery, at the top-left, is brightly decorated with pictures of animals. At the bottom-left is a small schoolroom. Can you see the cook, having a rest in the kitchen?

◀ *This doll's house shows what life was like in a big Victorian home.*

Tricks for the Eye

The Victorians loved magic tricks and **optical illusions** – tricks played on the eye. Many optical toys use something first described in 1824 called '**persistence of vision**'. This means that when we see an image, it stays with us for a fraction of a second. If we see two images very quickly, they seem to lie on top of one another.

▲ *A Victorian magic lantern show at a party – a special occasion for everyone.*

▼ *The* **zoetrope** *was another toy using 'persistence of vision'. As the drum spun round, the pictures inside seemed to move.*

The first toy to use this idea was the '**thaumatrope**,' or turning marvel, invented in 1826. You can make one of these yourself. Cut out a circle of card and make two holes at opposite edges – these are for two pieces of cotton. On one side of the card, draw a picture of a bird. On the other side, draw an upside-down cage. Hold the two pieces of cotton and blow on the card to make it spin. The bird is in the cage!

You can create many different trick pictures with a thaumatrope – a cow can jump over the Moon, or a chicken can ride a bicycle.

Magic Lantern Shows

The magic lantern was used to project, or throw, pictures painted on glass slides on to a wall. Overlapping slides were sometimes used to make the pictures move. Magic Lantern shows were a special treat for Victorian children.

In the 1890s, the ideas behind the **zoetrope** and the magic lantern were combined with another nineteenth-century invention – photography. The result was the cinema.

Toy Theatres

Some children had their own cardboard toy theatres. They put on short versions of pantomimes, such as *Aladdin*, and exciting adventure plays, such as *Three-fingered Jack, the Terror of Jamaica.* Scenes and characters were sold by the sheet, 'a penny plain and twopence coloured.' Children could paint and cut out the figures from the sheets. This toy theatre, complete with its own orchestra, is showing a play called *The Harlequinade*. It tells the story of a girl called Columbine who loves dancing in the open air. But her strict father, Pantaloon, wants her to stay indoors. Columbine meets and falls in love with a masked dancer called Harlequin. He helps her outwit her father and the two go off, dancing together.

▲ *Here Harlequin is saying to Columbine, 'Come dance with me my love. Will you be mine? Will you forever be my Columbine?'*

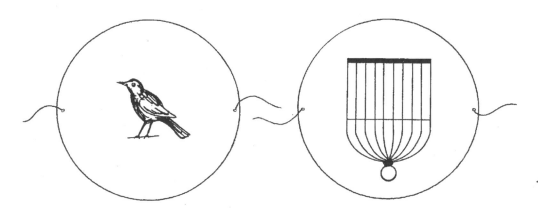

◄ *A thaumatrope.*

▲ A pull-along train set made in the 1800s.

Toy Trains

In the Victorian period, the whole of Britain was linked up by railway lines. The arrival of the steam train meant that, for the first time in history, people could travel faster than a running horse. It must have been very alarming going on a first train ride!

Children were fascinated by the new trains. A trip to a railway station was thrilling, with the wonderful hissing and clanking noises of the great engines. Back in the nursery, they wanted to play with toy trains. The early ones, made in the 1830s, were pull-along wooden toys. There were also metal trains, powered, like the real thing, by steam. These were called 'dribblers' because of the mess they left on the carpet. They were too dangerous for children to play with on their own.

▼ Some early flat soldiers and the box which they came in.

The most popular toy trains were driven by clockwork. They ran on rails, and a miniature railway line could be laid out across the nursery floor.

Toy Soldiers

The first toy soldiers were German 'flats', made from tin. Sometimes the Germans made rounded figures, but these were heavy and expensive because of all the metal they used.

In 1893, a British toy maker, William Britain, invented a way of making light, hollow, rounded soldiers. His whole family helped make the figures. His sons researched the uniforms of different regiments, and his daughters carefully painted each figure by hand.

C.W. Beaumont remembers Britain's soldiers:

'There was a definite thrill about the shiny red cardboard box in which they came, and another was provided when, the lid having been removed, one saw rows of soldiers fastened with a thread to a strip of cardboard ... The soldiers were lifted out and set up, one by one. How smart and fresh they looked in their shining uniforms and bright new paint.'

▼ *A teddy bear and an elephant who is dressed as a fashionable young man. Both are from the early 1900s, just after the Victorian period.*

Cuddly Toys

Soft toy animals were not produced in large numbers until the 1880s. The first teddy bears were made in the USA in 1903. The teddy bear got its name from the American president, Teddy Roosevelt, who refused to kill a bear cub while out hunting. They have stayed very popular since 1903.

Twentieth-Century Toys and Games

Children's games have changed more in the last 100 years than in any other period of history. In the early 1900s, you could still see children playing in the street with hoops, hobby horses and spinning tops, just as children had done since Roman times. These toys have now almost completely disappeared. What happened to make them so unpopular?

▲ *Children with homemade scooters in the East End of London. This was in 1933, when there were few cars in the streets.*

Scooters

In the early 1900s, toys with wheels, such as tricycles, rollerskates and scooters, made hoops and hobby horses seem old-fashioned. Scooters were a big craze after 1905. These were often homemade, using old pram wheels and bits of wood. Some parents would not let their children have them. Scooters were said to be dangerous, to wear out one shoe before the other, and to make children grow up lopsided.

Cars

In 1930, there were just one million cars in Britain; by 1970, there were 10 million. The rise of the motor car had a big effect on children's lives. Increased traffic made streets much less safe places to play. Children now depended on parks and playgrounds for their outdoor games.

Horses were no longer a common sight, and so children had less reason to ride hobby horses. They preferred to play with toy cars. These were first produced in about 1905, very soon after real cars started to appear. There were child-sized pedal cars and miniature metal cars.

In the 1960s, a ten-year-old boy described a game that he called 'road accidents':

'When we run about the playground pretending we are driving cars, we pretend that we are drunk, and go wobbling about the roads ... When someone crashes we send out a breakdown lorry. Sometimes the girls make a hospital ... and we get an ambulance to come out to fetch the injured drivers.'

▲ *An early pedal car zooms around the park. The other children look like they wish that they could have a go.*

The Hula Hoop

The hoop came back in a new form in 1958, as the hula hoop, which was swung around the hips. For two years, the hula hoop craze swept across Britain and the USA. The aim was to keep the hoop spinning on your hips as long as possible.

▼ *Playing with hoops in 1908.*

'The world hula hoop record does not belong to Gordon Boyd who has done 3,000. I have done 3,527 and my friend Billy has done 3,216.' –Tony Westrop, aged seven-and--a-half, 1960.

Cinema

In the 1930s, the most popular entertainment for children and adults was the cinema. Children went on Saturday afternoons to see cartoons, westerns and outer space serials, such as *Buck Rogers* and *Flash Gordon*. This is how one woman remembered those afternoons:

'Cowboy films were my favourite. We would cheer and boo and my cousin would jump up and down with excitement when the hero chased the villain at the end of the film.'

▲ *A Dan Dare ray gun from the 1950s. Like Buck Rogers, Dan Dare was a space hero. He appeared each week in the comic* Eagle, *fighting the green-skinned Treens from Venus.*

The weekly adventure serial at the pictures on a Saturday was imitated by children playing in the street. The popular games were 'cowboys and indians', and 'outer space' games, such as 'Buck Rogers'. The Buck Rogers space gun was one of the best selling toys of the 1930s.

Girls made up new singing games, based on American film stars like Shirley Temple and Betty Grable:

'I'm Shirley Temple, the girl with curly hair, I've got two dimples, and wear me skirts up there; I'm not able to do the Betty Grable, I'm Shirley Temple, the girl with curly hair.'

◄ *Shirley Temple was such a big film star in the 1930s that she had dolls made of her. Over 1 million Shirley Temple dolls were sold in 1934.*

An eleven-year-old girl described how this game was played:

'You all get in a giant ring – anybody can join in. There's somebody stands in the middle who is Shirley Temple, and the rest dance around singing. When they sing "two dimples," if you are Shirley Temple you push two fingers into your cheeks ...'

Television

Cinema became less popular in the 1950s as more and more people bought television sets. By 1964, 15 million homes had their own sets. Many parents worried that watching television would make children lazy. But, as with the cinema, children's television programmes led to new kinds of games.

In the 1950s, adventure serials set in the Middle Ages were popular, leading to games of 'Robin Hood' and 'William Tell'. In the 1960s, children all over Britain ran about with their arms

▼ *A family watches the blurry picture on their new television set.*

stretched out shouting, 'Exterminate! Exterminate!' They were pretending to be daleks, the terrifying robot monsters on the television series *Dr Who*.

Batman was a hugely popular series in 1966. Some children had their own Batman outfits and small, toy 'batmobiles'. Others pretended to be Batman and Robin by tying towels around their necks.

The Toy Industry

Television was a big help to the toy industry. As children's programmes became popular, new toys could be brought on to the market, linked with the programmes. The industry could also advertise its toys on Saturday morning television, when large numbers of children would be watching.

One effect of television was that children became bored more quickly with their toys. Once *Thunderbirds* started broadcasting, toys based on the earlier programmes, *Stingray* and *Fireball XL5*, seemed old-fashioned.

New materials, especially plastic, made toys much cheaper. For the first time, rich and poorer children were playing with the same types of toys, such as plastic guns and Barbie dolls.

▼ *A 1959 Barbie doll, dressed in the latest French fashions.*

Barbie, Ken, Sindy and Paul

In the late 1950s, teenagers became a separate group, with their own pop music, fashions, films and magazines. This was reflected by the American teenage doll, Barbie, who appeared in 1959. Barbie came with her own way of life, explained in comics and television adverts. She soon had a boyfriend too, called Ken.

Barbie was beautiful, popular and incredibly talented. She could dance, swim, ride a horse, drive a car and cook. In 1961, Barbie made a record:

'I never bothered with romance,
Or gave any boy a second glance,
and then, I met Ken.'

She was popular with young girls, who loved dressing her up in her different outfits. Barbie and Ken were so successful that they were copied by British toy makers, who created Sindy and Paul.

Action Man

Meanwhile, boys had their own doll which they could play with and dress up. He was called Action Man. He was about the same size as Barbie, but he had jointed limbs that all moved. Thanks to these, he could be placed in any position. Action Man came with many different military costumes and weapons. He could be a soldier, a scuba-diver or a pilot, complete with a working parachute. He had a small scar on his cheek to make him look tough.

▲ *Like the Roman gladiator doll on page 6, Action Man is a boy's fighting doll with moving limbs. Here he is on display at a 1966 British toy fair.*

You can make almost anything with Lego, the plastic building bricks invented in Denmark. The name comes from the Danish word, leg, meaning play.

Power Rangers and Biker Mice from Mars

One of the most popular children's television series of 1994 was *Biker Mice from Mars*, a cartoon starring muscular mice who battle against the evil fish-faced Plutarkians. Children could re-live the programme with toy Biker Mice and Plutarkians.

▲ *Stand aside stinky Plutarkians, here come the Biker Mice from Mars!*

In 1995, the Mice were overtaken in popularity by another television programme, *Mighty Morphin Power Rangers*. The Rangers are 'five ordinary teenagers' who have been chosen to save the world from Rita Repulsa and her evil Space Aliens. They do this by calling on the spirits of ancient dinosaurs and transforming into superheroes.

Each week, the teenagers fight a different strange Space Alien, such as a giant two-headed parrot, a sting-shooting 'grumble bee', or a 'food-gobbling pudgy pig'. The programme was so successful that it was made into a film. The toy shops filled up with Rangers and evil Space Alien dolls.

▼ *A portable computer game system, with Sonic the Hedgehog on the screen.*

Computer Games

Computer games were invented in the 1970s. To begin with, they were very simple. You had to bounce a ball across the screen or shoot down a moving target using a special control panel. Christopher Stamper, who grew up to design his own games, remembers :

'I was hooked right from the first ping-pong games. For the first time, I could control something on a television screen.'

The games soon became much more complicated. Characters were introduced, such as *Sonic the Hedgehog* and *Super Mario*. Both were so successful that they were given their own cartoon series.

Donkey Kong Country

The game *Donkey Kong Country*, released in 1994, sold over
7 million copies in one year. It features a gorilla who has to find
his hoard of bananas, stolen by evil creatures called Kremlings.
To find all the bananas, he must explore over a hundred secret
'worlds', avoiding booby traps and obstacles. Eleven-year-old
William Evans, from London, explained why he loved the game:

'The **graphics** are the best ever ... The other good thing about it
is that there are two objectives ... one to complete the game, but
also to find all the secret worlds.'

Many adults are worried by the popularity of computer games.
They say that children ought to be outside in the fresh air, playing
traditional street games. These games taught children how to get
on with each other and gave them plenty of exercise. But children
playing computer games might spend too much time on their own
and become unfit. What do you think?

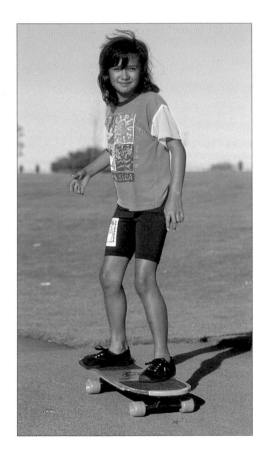

◀ *Despite television and
computer games, many
children still get plenty of
exercise in the open air,
playing with skateboards
and bikes.*

Timeline

2000 BC Spinning tops used by the ancient Egyptians.	**1120** Bartholomew Fair, a famous fair for toys, founded in London, England.	**1413** First professional doll maker recorded in Nuremburg, Germany.	**1558** Earliest-recorded dolls' house, made for Duke Albrecht V of Bavaria.	**1640** Athanasius Kircher first describes the magic lantern.

1762 John Spilsbury sells 'dissected maps', the first jigsaws.	**1826** Thaumatrope (turning marvel) invented.	**1834** Zoetrope (wheel of life) invented. 	**1835** Germans began making toy trains, at first out of wood.

1895 First cinema opens in Paris.	**1901** Frank Hornby produces the Meccano construction set.	**1903** First teddy bears made in America.	**1905** Child-size toy cars made. 

1644
Parliament bans maypole dancing as 'a heathenish vanity'.

1647
Parliament bans Christmas celebrations.

1672
Clockwork toy soldiers made in Nuremburg, Germany.

1760
Andreas Hilpert of Coburg mass-produces 'flats', flat tin soldiers.

1849
Cockfighting banned in Britain.

1850s
First rubber toys made, such as bouncing balls.

1870
Celluloid, an early type of plastic invented.

1889
Tiddlywinks invented.

1893
William Britain makes rounded, hollow tin soldiers.

1936
Television broadcasts begin in the London area.

1958
The hula-hoop craze sweeps through Britain and the USA.

1959
Barbie doll created.

1970s
First computer games produced.

Glossary

Clockwork
A device based on clock machinery for making a toy move. The device inside the toy has a spring, tightly wound up by a key. As the spring unwinds, it turns the wheels that move the toy.

Composition
A mixture of soaked paper, plaster, flour or glue. This mixture was poured into moulds to form dolls' heads.

Festival
A celebration, usually held to mark a religious event, or important times of the year, such as the arrival of spring or the end of the harvest.

Graphics
The pictures in a computer game.

Guilds
Societies formed by craftspeople or traders, for helping each other.

Hobby horses
Toy horses which were made by attaching a stick to a wooden horse's head.

Holy days
Special days for religious worship, such as a Sunday or a saint's day. In the Middle Ages, people went to Church on holy days and then played games.

Lathes
Machines for shaping wood. The wood is shaped by moving it against a cutting tool.

Maypole
An upright pole or tree trunk, set in the village centre and decorated with flowers and ribbons. People celebrated May Day by dancing around a maypole.

Morris dancing
A traditional dance. Morris dancers wore bright costumes decorated with bells, and danced with sticks.

Optical illusions
Tricks which deceive the eye.

Persistence of vision
The experience of seeing an image for a fraction of a second after it has gone.

Puritan

Member of a sixteenth and seventeenth-century religious group. Puritans wanted to make Christian worship purer and simpler, and to live their lives in strict agreement with teachings in the Bible.

Thaumatrope

A spinning disc, which makes one picture appear on top of another.

Zoetrope

A spinning metal drum containing pictures, which tricks the eye into believing the images in the pictures arc moving.

Books to Read

Oxlade, C: *Toys through Time* (Macdonald Young Books, 1995)

Siliprandi, K: *Toys and Games* (Wayland, 1994)

Tanner, G and Wood, T: *Toys* (A & C Black, 1993)

Thomson, R: *Toys and Games* (Franklin Watts, 1992)

Index

advertising 25, 40
animal toys 6, 20

ball games 5
Batman 39
Belgium 16
board games 15, 31
building blocks 31

cartoons 38, 42
child labour 23
cinema 32, 38
clockwork toys 21,
  34
computer games 42–43
  Donkey Kong Country 43
  Sonic the Hedgehog 42
  Super Mario 42
cuddly toys 35

die 8, 9
dolls' houses 31
doll maker 20, 21
dolls 5, 6, 8, 17, 20,
  Action Man 7, 41
  Barbie 40, 41
  gladiator **6**, 7
  Sindy 40

factories 22, 30
fairs 13, 20, 24
festivals 8, 12
  Christmas 13, 19, 20

Easter 12, 13
May Day 13
Saturnalia 8, 9
Shrove Tuesday 14, 19
St John's Eve 13
Yule 12
football 14, 19

games
  blindman's buff 12
  bucca 11, 17
  clapping 27, 28
  cockstride 17
  hide and seek 26
  knucklebones 10, 16, 17
  leapfrog 12
  let's pretend 17
  old man in the well 28,
    29
  thread the needle 26
  tug of war 26
  winter 14
Germany 12, 20, 22–24, 34

hobby horses 13,17, 24, 36
hoops 7, 36, 37

jigsaw puzzles 31

materials
  bone 6
  feathers 5
  horsehair 5

plastic 40
pottery 6, 8
soaked paper 22
wood 5, 6, 20, 22, 24

Noah's Ark 23
nursery 30, 31, 34

optical toys 32

Power Rangers 42
Puritans 18, 19

roller skates 36

scooters 36
skipping 28, **29**
spinning tops 7, 17, 36
street pedlars 24

teddy bears 35
television 39, 40, 42
The Netherlands 16, 24
toy
  cars 36, 37
  makers 20–25, 35, 40
  shops 24, 25, 42
  soldiers 21, 34, 35
  theatres 33
  trains 34
tricycles 36

westerns 38